DON'T CRUSH THAT DWARF, HAND ME THE PLIERS was first performed at the Whidbey Island Center For the Arts on March 26, 2005. It was an Otherworld Media Production. The cast and creative contributors were:

GEORGE LEROY TIREBITER............................ David Ossman
THE JANITOR & JOE BEETS .... Mark Therien
DEACON E L MOUSE & PICO .... Michael McInerny
SISTER FLASH, MOM & MRS PRESKY .... Sandy O'Brien
JERRY YARROW & ALVARADO .... Halim Dunsky
GEORGE TIREBITER (playing PORGIE,
LT TIREBITER & DANNY DOLLAR).............. Orson Ossman
BEN BLAND .... George Henny
DAD .... Roy Feiring
PRINCIPAL POOP .... Jim Scullen
BOTTLES .... Marissa Wilhelm
TELEVISION PERSONALITIES .... Deana Duncan
T V PERSONALITIES & PRIVATE .... Bif Dangerfield
MISS AMES... Ahna Dunn-Wilder
MARIE .... Christina Atkinson
THE ANDROID SISTERS, HAWAIIAN
SELL-OUT GIRLS, CHEERLEADERS....... Christina Atkinson,
   Ahna Dunn-Wilder, Kate Hodges, Marissa Wilhelm

Adaptation & direction .... David Ossman
Music .... Rick Ingrasci
Set design & construction .... Jim Scullen
Technical director... Tod Ackley
Producer.. Judith Walcutt

SETTING

DON'T CRUSH THAT DWARF takes place in Los Angeles, at the end of the 20th century, in George Leroy Tirebiter's small Laurel Canyon bungalow where he has lived for thirty years or more.

Tirebiter, a retired B-Movie and radio actor, awake at 4 A M and hungry for a pizza place that delivers, watches himself in various guises, including roles in two different movies, showing on his late-night T V.

High School Madness features the young actor George as "Porgie" who, with his buddy "Mudhead," is trying to locate his stolen High School so he can graduate. *Parallel Hell* finds "Lt. Tirebiter" trying to escape the killing in a gritty war drama. The two films, with commercial interruptions, channel-surf through George's memory, until his twin movie personalities are simultaneously put on trial for being subversively un-American in a time of Declared Emergency as the movie studio itself is auctioned off around them.

Based on The Firesign Theatre's most famous comedy album, released in 1970 and collected as a classic audio production by the Library of Congress, DON'T CRUSH THAT DWARF, HAND ME THE PLIERS is a surreal blend of media, historical eras and satirical comedy directed at both American politics and Tinsel-Town show business.

THE FIRESIGN THEATRE'S "DON'T CRUSH THAT DWARF, HAND ME THE PLIERS!"

adapted for the stage by
David Ossman
original audioscript by
Philip Austin, Peter Bergman,
David Ossman &
Phil Proctor

BROADWAY PLAY PUBLISHING INC
New York
www.broadwayplaypublishing.com
info@broadwayplaypublishing.com

First printing: May 2012
I S B N: 978-0-88145-524-3

Book design: Marie Donovan
Page make-up: Adobe Indesign
Typeface: Palatino
Printed and bound in the U S A

(A T V screen-shaped frame occupies upstage center, mounted on a riser with the edges concealed by curtains. It is within this frame that the television and movie action begins. The area is brightly lit when the T V is turned on by the JANITOR *at the beginning of the play.)*

(The stage is set as GEORGE TIREBITER'S *apartment, with a lounge-chair and a small side-table down right. The table is set with a T V remote, a phone book, a phone and the novel* GEORGE *has fallen asleep reading.)*

(There's a larger two-person dining table with a couple of café chairs center left, and up left stands an old refrigerator.)

(The lights come dimly up on the playing area and we find GEORGE *dozing in his bathrobe in his lounge chair.)*

(A JANITOR *enters from right, sweeping the stage before him with a push broom. He gets to center, stops and looks out at the audience.)*

JANITOR: You folks got some troubles here? Organ trouble? Eleck-trical difficulties? You been "Waitin' fer the Electrician?" Humph! I can get yer iron lung workin' again! *(He leans his broom against a chair and takes the T V remote from the side-table.)* I sure can't figure out why you people seem to think this thing is magic. *(He holds it up to demonstrate.)* It's just this little chromium switch here...

(When JANITOR *presses the remote, the "screen" lights up, revealing* DEACON MOUSE, *pitching silently to his revival congregation.)*

JANITOR: Ya know what they say: "Don't crush that dwarf, my friends," *(He gestures toward the screen.)* "Hand me the pliers." *(He holds up the remote.)* Use the tool, fool! *(He sets the remote down and picks up his broom.)* My, my. You folks are so superstitious! *(He sweeps almost all the way out, then goes back and picks up the remote again.)* I guess I gotta take off the mute.

*(*JANITOR *does so and immediately* DEACON MOUSE *can be heard, tapping on his microphone. Now we can hear the organ music swelling as well.* GEORGE *dozes in his lounge-chair.)*

DEACON MOUSE: ...'icrophone 'orking? *(Tap tap)* Is it going to be All Right?

(From behind DEACON MOUSE, *the excited* CONGREGATION *responds:)*

CONGREGATION: It's going to be All Right!

*(*DEACON MOUSE *steps out of the screen and comes down center, laughing and jolly, the Hot Dog Deacon. The* CONGREGATION *follows.)*

DEACON MOUSE: Ha Ha! You bet, Dear Friends! It is going to be All Right! It's going to be All Right tonight, here at the Powerhouse Church of the Presumptuous Assumption of the Blinding Light!

*(*DEACON MOUSE, *along with the* CONGREGATION*)*

DEACON MOUSE & CONGREGATION:
Oh, blinding light! Oh, light that blinds!
I cannot, cannot see...!
The sun's behind the moon's bright shine—
Who will look out for me?
Look out! Look out that Space-Hole Tube
To see the Eye of God!
You know for sure He's watching You!
His only, lonely job!

(The CONGREGATION *applauds him with shouts of "Yes, yes!" and "Right, Rev!" and "It's His Job!")*

DEACON MOUSE: Yes, Dear Friends, welcome to Sister Flash's Hour of Reckoning. I'm Deacon E L Mouse. But, Dear Friends, in these days of Modern Time, when you can't tell the A Cs from the D Cs, well, aren't we all yearning for a little Stopping Power? Dear Friends, I mean a Smokey Glass. Don't you think I mean a Lightning Rod with which to chase the Spooks away? Don't you know I mean our own Sister Flash? She's been up for a week, but she's coming down!

(The right balcony [if possible] is spotlight. It's set to look like an old bi-plane with SISTER FLASH *in the cockpit, scarf trailing in the wind. The plane engine drones.* SISTER FLASH's *airy voice comes in as if "on the radio.")*

SISTER FLASH: Hello, Dear Friends! It's so beautiful up here, Dear Friends. It's so clean. Yes, Dear Friends, there's no drunken drivers here. No broken glass. No air. Over.

DEACON MOUSE: *(With tremendous B-movie melodrama)* White Lightning! White Lightning! This is Ground Beef Control. Do you read me?

SISTER FLASH: I read only Good Books. Over.

DEACON MOUSE: Roger! You must be way Out There, Sister!

SISTER FLASH: I'm high, alright, but not on false drugs. I'm high on the real thing! Powerful gasoline, a clean windshield and shiny, shiny shoes! Over... We're turning over!

*(*SISTER FLASH *mimes a sudden argument with her co-pilot. She is in great peril. The bi-plane engine roars!)*

DEACON MOUSE: She's turning over!

SISTER FLASH: *(Fighting the demons)* Get Thee behind me!

DEACON MOUSE: Are you in danger, Sister?

SISTER FLASH: *(Recovering)* I'm all right.

DEACON MOUSE: Roger!

SISTER FLASH: *(Correcting herself)* I'm all right, <u>Roger</u>. Just a little argument with my co-pilot. And guess what, Rog? The little red needle's pointing to "E"— and, while that's always stood for Excelent in my Book, I guess it means I'm Out Of Gas. You'll have to sing me in, Dear Friends. My favorite. Hymn 1517...

(The plane takes a nose-dive, its motor straining. A tiny figure with a parachute jumps, the 'chute pops open and slowly falls to the stage during the song.)

(Music is at the back of this book)

CONGREGATION: *(Singing)*
We're marching, marching to Shibboleth,
With the Eagle and the Sword!
We're praising Zion 'til her death,
Until we meet our last reward!

MEN: Our Lord's reward!

WOMEN: Zion! Oh happy Zion!
O'er wrapped, but not detained!

MEN: Lion! Oh, f'rocious Lion!
His beard our mighty mane!

WOMEN: At First and Main!

MEN: Oh, we'll go marching, marching to Omaha,
With the Buckram and the Cord!

WOMEN: You'll hear us "boom" our State!

MEN: Ha ha! As we cross the final ford!

WOMEN: The flaming Ford!

ALL: Zion! O, mighty Zion!
Your bison now are dust!
As your cornflakes rise
'Gainst the rust-red skies,
Then our blood requires us must
Go...

MEN: Marching, marching to Shibboleth,
With the Eagle and the...

WOMEN: The Buckram and the Cord!

MEN: Sword! Praising Zion 'til her death!

WOMEN: Ha ha!

MEN: Until we eat our last reward!

WOMEN: The flaming Ford

ALL: Zion! O, righteous Zion!
There is no one to blame!
For the homespun pies
'Neath the cracking skies
Shall release the fulsome rain!

TENOR: Shall release!

MEN: Shall release!

SOPRANO: Shall release!

WOMEN: Shall release!

ALL: Shall release the vinyl rain!

(Some time during the hymn, GEORGE comes awake, aware
that his T V is on. He sits up, rubs his eyes and watches the
CONGREGATION singing. [The T V is always in front of
GEORGE, even though the "screen" is to his rear.] SISTER
FLASH finally lands on stage as the Hymn ends. It's all an
effect—she really runs in, scarf trailing and the organ music
rapturous.)

SISTER FLASH: I'm down! Thank you, Dear Friends, I'm
down, I'm grounded, safe and sound, trailing clouds of

glory, I'm down. And I'm marching! Yes, Dear Friends,
I'm marching to Dinner! Because I'm Hungry! Yes, I'm
Hungry! Safe and sound and Hungry!

CONGREGATION: We're Hungry!

(GEORGE *gets up and stretches.*)

GEORGE: I'm hungry...

SISTER FLASH: Of course you're Hungry! I'm Hungry!
We're all Hungry! So, Let's Eat!

CONGREGATION: Let's Eat!

(GEORGE *is totally amused by what he's watching and joins
in.*)

GEORGE: Let's eat!

SISTER FLASH: And we said the Word!

CONGREGATION: What was it?

GEORGE: Yes, what was it?

SISTER FLASH: And we ate it! Hot Dog! And what was
the word?

CONGREGATION & GEORGE: Hot Dog!

(GEORGE *has watched enough. He reaches for his remote.
It's not where he left it. He finds it on the table.*)

SISTER FLASH: Hot Dog! Yes, Dear Friends, a mighty
Hot Dog is our Lord! I'm not talking about Hate! No!
I'm talking about Ate! Dinner at Eight! Let's Eat!

CONGREGATION: More sugar!

(GEORGE *flicks off the T V with the remote. The "screen"
goes dark.*)

GEORGE: More sugar and mad cow disease—the perfect
T V diet! Well, it certainly makes me hungry... (*Checks
his watch*) Mickey's little hands say—it's four in the
morning. Oh, my... (*He crosses up to check inside the
'fridge*) Hmmm... Thai Food Mary's— "it's contagious"

....Green maraschino cherries—what was I drinking?...
Laughing Cow cheese...some things never change.
*(He takes out a little Cow cheese, unwraps it and nibbles as
he checks out the freezer)* My God! *(He pulls out a frozen
baggy)* These 'shrooms must be thirty years old! Makes
my mouth dry just to think about it. *(Puts the baggy
back)* Let's see what else is on...

*(GEORGE goes back to his chair and flicks the remote while
he finishes his cheese. ARNIE appears on the screen.)*

ARNIE: ...urrounded by a thin, thin, 16-millimeter shell.
And, inside, it's delicious! Arnie's whole Beef Halves.
We deliver! Thirsty?

GEORGE: That's me.

ARNIE: Wouldn't you like some of this Old Filipino
Creamy, comin' in Shorts and Quarts? And Tubs of
slaw!

GEORGE: I'll take two.

ARNIE: Sorry, pal. Only one Tub per coustomer. That's
Whole Beef Halves—We Deliver. Everywhere! This
offer not good in Sectors R or N.

GEORGE: They never deliver up in the Hills anyway...

*(He flicks the remote. There on the screen is GEORGE's
double, gray hair, moustache and all.)*

GEORGE ON T V: Remember me? I'm George Tirebiter,
former celebrity.

GEORGE: Good God! That's me!

GEORGE ON T V: Well, even if you don't remember me
from the Golden Days of Hollywood, I've come back!
Back to LIFE, with Preparation B-plus. A low-impact,
metabolically-neutral combination of buzz-words and
banana-oil that reduces the physical symptoms of
paranoia and delusional thinking so fast, it's scary! Just
watch...

GEORGE: Just watch! Who could watch that? I look terrible!

(Again, GEORGE flicks the remote and the TV is off.)

GEORGE: Why do I do these things? Ah. The money. The makeup kid wanted me to "look as young as you feel, Mister T." It's even worse than that dog food commercial—"cats and dogs . . ." Yeach! *(He picks up the phonebook.)* I'm starving! *(He hunts thru the phonebook.)* Let's see... Ocelots... Paupers... Pipenipples... Polombras... Pizzas! O K... "Hank's Hawaiian Juggerknot—extreme pineapple"... "New Leviathon— Whale of a Slice"... "Nick's No Anchovies, Ever! Pizza—Mystery Toppings! We deliver!" Ah! *(He dials.)* Good evening, yes. I'd like to... I'd like to be on hold, yes, indeedy!... I love this station... No announcers, no music, no nothing. Very Zen... "I'm so-o-o tired, I haven't slept a wink... Hello! Yes, this is George Tirebiter, Camden N 200-R. I want to order a no-anchovy pizza to go...no delivery in the hills without an armed escort? But my dear, what about for a former Hollywood Celebrity? ...I can hire you as MY escort? Somehow, I don't... Well, thank you anyhow. *(He puts down the phone. Sits for a moment. He takes off his glasses and rubs his eyes, then puts them back on and looks around, remembering.)* What was I... ? Yes, I was reading my book, then Ben Bland's All-Night Matinee came on. Ben was telling me about the scandalous life of my ex-wife, Barbara The Bitch. If he only knew the real story! Then the power went out. I dozed off in my chair... woke up when the power came back on... Oh, Sister, I'm hungry!

(GEORGE flicks the remote back on. The full stage lights up and we are back in the Hour of Reckoning. SISTER FLASH is preaching, the CONGREGATION is chiming in. DEACON MOUSE is distributing food. GEORGE is suddenly in the middle of it all.)

SISTER: Come on up to Sister Flash if you want to eat! Come on up, darling. Don't be afraid. I won't bite you! But you can bite me!

GEORGE: Weird. Must be an overload of my Digi-Sat TV. And they said 3-D was years in the future!... It's just too much!

SISTER: Is it really too much, Dear Friend? Well, look at this! *(She pulls open his fridge and points out box after box of fast-food leftovers.)* Look at this steaming heap! Too much of Admirable Byrd's crackly-brown French-fried chicken fingers? Too many cuts of Mother Baker's Deep-Dish Sheep Dip Cherrystone Pie? Too many Tubs O' Slaw?

DEACON MOUSE: How about it, George? Are there ever too many Tubs O' Slaw?

CONGREGATION: *(Advancing on George with more Tubs)* Take my Tub!

SISTER: Dip deep, darling!

DEACON MOUSE: Take some pot-buttered groat clusters!

SISTER: Well, here you are!

(GEORGE is surrounded by buckets of food. He grabs something.)

GEORGE: My god! This is amazing! I'm interactive! Oh! It's still warm! *(He dips into a couple of buckets and chews on some groat-clusters.)*

SISTER: Say thank you!

GEORGE: Thank you! Thank you!

SISTER: Not with your mouth full! I'll talk—you eat!

CONGREGATION: Hot dog! Let's eat!

(Led by DEACON MOUSE, the CONGREGATION leaves via the T V screen, chanting their creed.)

GEORGE: Oh, yes, I'm eating!

SISTER: And while you eat, be assured Dear Friend, that one of the Two Greatest Guys in the Universe—that great Guy Upstairs—is thanking me, as you are thanking me.

GEORGE: Thank you...

SISTER: Doesn't that change your heart, Dear Friend?

GEORGE: Yes, it certainly does...

SISTER: Don't you feel your heart burning?

GEORGE: Oh, I can feel it burn!

SISTER: Can you feel the change? Aren't you full? Don't you feel the Changes, Dear Friend?

GEORGE: I do. Of course I do...

SISTER: I feel you changing, George! *(To the Audience)* Isn't he changing...

(Overlapping SISTER FLASH's line, as he strides off the T V screen and down stage, is T V host JERRY YARROW. SISTER FLASH discretely makes her exit. T V theme music plays.)

JERRY: ...Changing With The Times! Hi, everybody! I'm Jerry Yarrow and I'm ready to meet our next Famous Fall Guy! Winner of the Academy's coveted Good Sport Award in 1956, he put his art in cans from Canada to Kashmir when Tinsel Town was young—but he's not! Welcome George Leroy Tirebiter!

(GEORGE is still wearing his bathrobe. The spotlight is on him. How did he get on a game show? Right. The money. He walks "on camera," gathering his professional presence.)

JERRY: Hubba, hubba, George! What a suit! Well, it's nice to see you looking like you're back on your feet again, George, and ready to play our little game again.

GEORGE: *(Shucking off the bathrobe)* Thank you very much, Jerry.

JERRY: George, first a tip for our viewers, maybe. How does an old man like you stay alive?

GEORGE: Well, Jerry, I try to get up every morning and watch television all day.

JERRY: Do you have a special diet, George?

GEORGE: Well, I don't eat...

JERRY: You don't eat?

GEORGE: No. But it hasn't affected my appetite!

JERRY: Ha ha! It hasn't affected his...

GEORGE: I don't suppose you'd have any hot mustard for these groat clusters, do you?

JERRY: Funny guy, funny, funny guy. Well, you won't be able to eat in a minute, George, after you Turn Your Back and get ready for this truly scary Stab From The Past!

(A truly scary musical chord)

GEORGE: Do I really have to?

JERRY: You really have to, George. Now, do you remember those incredibly loveable, incredibly stupid *Porgie & Mudhead* movies you made back in the Fifties?

GEORGE: Haven't seen one in years. Ralph Spoilsport used to sponsor them, but he lost his lease—and I don't get a penny in residuals, you know...

JERRY: Cut the data dump, George, and tell me— What are you going to do when the original "Bottles," Mudhead's crazy, hopped-up girlfriend drops straight through that Celebrity Trap Door?

GEORGE: No! You can't do that! It's my ex-wife! She's trying to kill me!

(GEORGE knows what he must do. He grabs the remote off his side table and clicks it on to the next channel. A

succession of different program bits appear on T V as he clicks the remote.)

BEARWHIZ BEER GUY: See that bear lappin' up that good ol' country water? Sure makes a big, hairy guy like me thirsty. That's when I wrap my lips around a tall, sweaty, edible bottle of good ol' country Bear Whiz Beer. As my ol' Pappy use to say, "It's in the water, that's why it yaller." Aaaah! Bear Whiz! A liquid product of Andy Beerwhitz Brewery, Animal, Mo...

(GEORGE clicks on to the next channel.)

MADGE: ...'resident of the World Bank, and you still find the time to make the nicest Peccary Pie in all of Lompox. Oh, Darlene! I remember when the least little problem use to put you right to sleep! How...

(GEORGE clicks on.)

HIPPIE GEORGE: *(Decked out in tie-dye and head-band)...* not in any way want to put myself in a confrontatory position either with the United Snakes, or with Them. And you can believe me, because I never lie, and I'm always right. So wake up and take a look at your only logical choice. Me. George Tirebiter.

T V ANNOUNCER: Paid for by Tirebiter for Political Solutions Committee, Sector R. This is U-T V, for You, The Viewer.

(GEORGE watches his younger, long-haired self with some scorn. Late Show theme music introduces the Movie Host on screen.)

BEN: Hello. I'm Ben Bland with your Howl of the Wolf Movie! Presenting honest stories of working people, as told by rich Hollywood stars. This early morning's whacky feature stars Porgie & Mudhead in *High School Madness*, with Dave Casman as Porgie and Joe Bertman as Mudhead, with a great supporting cast—Spring Byington, Broderick Crawford and George Spelvyn.

It's the third in a great funny series, released in 1-9-5-0. Here's *High School Madness* from Paranoid Pictures.

(GEORGE *is delighted and takes a seat in the first row of the audience. He is completely taken by this movie from his past and watches intently as it unfolds around him, in his Technicolor living room, which becomes the* TIREBITER *family's breakfast nook.*)

(*After a big studio fanfare, the* ANDROID SISTERS *appear on screen to sing the movie's title song.*)

ANDROID SISTERS: (*Singing*)
Porgie Tirebiter!
He's a spy and a girl delighter!
Orgie Firefighter!
He's a student like you.
If you're lookin' for a Captain of the Ring Ball Team,
You can bet he won't be there!
You'll find him pa-popping off at Pop's Sodium Shop
Trailin' a Red with red hair!
Doobie-doo-wa!
Porgie Tirebiter!
Just a student like you!

(PORGIE, *a 1950 High School senior, runs in:*)

PORGIE: Like me?

ANDROID SISTERS: Just a student like you!

(DAD, *an ex-W W II Marine if there ever was one, comes on, spoiling for a fight.*)

DAD: Stop singing and finish your homework!

ANDROID SISTERS: (*The Big Finish*) Just a student like you!

(*The* ANDROID SISTERS *make their exit and* MOM *enters through the T V screen with plates in her hands, which she sets on the table.*)

MOM: Adolph! Come and get it! Your clam cakes are getting damp!

(DAD *enters, armed and ready for anything.*)

DAD: *(Dusting himself off)* 10-4 Eleanor! Whew! Defoliating a Victory Garden certainly does work up an appetite!

MOM: You sit right down, Father, and dig right in!

DAD: By this afternoon, I'll start digging the Pit. If I can get some work out of that boy of yours, I can have the bunker finished by Election Day.

MOM: Why, here he is now, Fred.

DAD: Stop calling me Fred. My name's Adolph.!

PORGIE: *(Coming on, combing his hair)* Bombs away, Dad. Morning, Mom! Hot dog! Groat cakes again! Heavy on the 30-weight, Mom.

DAD: Don't eat with your hands, son. Use your entrenching tool.

PORGIE: *(Gorging on his food)* Aw, gee, Dad! I'm just trying to save time. It isn't every day a guy graduates from High School!

DAD: How many times have I heard that before?

MOM: Well, you boys fight it out among yourselves.

DAD: O K, Mother.

(DAD *lays* PORGIE *out with a sucker punch. They struggle on the floor as* MOM *dithers around with her pocket book.*)

MOM: Oh, my! Look at the time! I've got to dress for my bridge club.

PORGIE: *(Struggling)* Gee, Mom! Isn't that bridge built yet?

DAD: No, Son! *(Punches him)* And it won't be, until free hands on both sides of the Big Ditch can press the same button at the same time. *(Pow!)*

PORGIE: O K, Dad! I give! Ow! Oh, boy! Whew! Can I eat my breakfast now?

DAD: Only if you stay out of trouble, boy! Your shenanigans could cost me this election.

PORGIE: Aw, come on, Dad. No Irishman can stop you from getting to be Dog Killer this time. *(His mouth full)* You're a natural!

MOM: Don't wolf your food!

(From outside, the ah-ooo-gah of a jalopy horn.)

PORGIE: Oh oh! There's Mudhead! Graduation, here I come! So long, Dad! Keep 'em flying!

(PORGIE scrambles up from the table and runs up "on screen," where he meets MUDHEAD.)

DAD: Oh, that son of mine!

MOM: He's not your son, Fred.

(MOM leaves, followed hopelessly by DAD.)

DAD: Stop torturing me, Ethyl.

(As DAD leaves, so does GEORGE, from where he has been sitting, watching his movie. MUDHEAD, at the wheel of his noisy jalopy, picks up PORGIE and they continue their ride to High School "on screen.")

PORGIE: Come on! Step on it, Mudhead!

MUDHEAD: Aw, I'd love to, Porgie, but I've got my two-tones through the floorboards already!

PORGIE: Well, O K. Then we could take the shortcut through Frogtown.

MUDHEAD: Aw reet! We can stop off at Pop's and dig some jugs!

PORGIE: Some what?

MUDHEAD: That Louise Wong's got a balcony you could do Shakespeare from!

PORGIE: Aw, not now, Mudhead. They need me at the last meeting of the Philatelist's Club.

MUDHEAD: Gee, Porge...I didn't know you masturbated.

PORGIE: Creepies, Mudhead! Where's your school spirit?

MUDHEAD: In the rumble seat. Want a snort?

PORGIE: Very funny.

MUDHEAD: Sure is.

PORGIE: Gee, everybody at Morse Science High has an extra-curricular activity but you.

MUDHEAD: Doesn't Louise count?

PORGIE: Only to ten, Mudhead. You know, that's just it.

MUDHEAD: Just what?

PORGIE: Well, we're the leaders of Tomorrow.

MUDHEAD: Yeah, but it's Today!

PORGIE: But what are you going to do Tomorrow— after we graduate?

MUDHEAD: Oh, well, I thought maybe I'd go out and find a bunch of guys who dress alike and follow 'em around.

PORGIE: What, you?

MUDHEAD: Or, I could go out and pick up a couple of girls!

PORGIE: Oh, is that all you think about? Picking up things? Gollee, Mudhead! Don't you remember what Principal Poop put down at the Pep Rally yesterday?

MUDHEAD: Principal Who... . ?

(Now, in a movie-like "wipe," the boys fade out as the
ANDROID SISTERS *return to the stage as* CHEERLEADERS.
They treat the theater audience like highschoolers.)

CHEERLEADERS: P-E-P! P-E-P! Mooo-oooooore Pep Pills!
(Faster and faster) Pep Pills! Pep Pills! Pep Pills!... Yaaay!
(Big Finish) Pep Pilllls!

(The CHEERLEADERS *stand aside, an enthusiastic audience*
for PRINCIPAL POOP, *who makes his perpetually befuddled*
way down stage to a waiting microphone. POOP *taps on the*
*microphone unsurely. A guy in the audience [*ALVARADO*]*
makes rude noises.)

POOP: Is this on? Thank you, fellow kids. *(Shushing*
ALVARADO*)* Quiet! In addressing for the assembling
this morning...

ALVARADO: *(From the audience)* Fuck you!

POOP: Thank you! Er, I am recalling the words of our
Foundry—er, Founder of Morse Science—Ukaipah
Heap—who pressed the first bricks with his own
hands...

ALVARADO: Who cares?

POOP: "Knowledge for the pupil—uh, the People!"
he said. "Give them a light and they'll follow it
anywhere." We think that is a fair and a wise guy—er,
rule to be guided by...

ALVARADO: What is reality?

POOP: And we're not afraid of it, are we?

ALVARADO: Eat it!

POOP: You bet!

ALVARADO: Eat it raw!

POOP: Rah, rah, rah! That's the spirits we have here! So
come on, kids!

ALVARADO: *(Leaving the hall, he calls back halfheartedly)* Fuck you!

POOP: Line up, sign up and re-enlist today! Because we need more schooling for more students for Morse Science High!

ALVARADO: *(Almost out)* Boooo!

POOP: *(Saluting the boooos)* Thank you.

ALVARADO: *(One last one)* Boooo!

POOP: *(Following him out, under his breath)* Fuck you, too!

(This Flashback fades away as the CHEERLEADERS *follow* POOP *out with a few cheers.)*

CHEERLEADERS: Morse Science! Morse Science! Lots more Science at Morse Science High!

*(*PORGIE *and* MUDHEAD *reappear in the jalopy.)*

PORGIE: So you see, Mudhead? It's like the Pooper said—with counter-subversive educational priorities the way they are, well, it really helps our side to re-enlist!

MUDHEAD: Is that what you're gonna do?

PORGIE: Hell no! Right after I graduate, I'm gonna cut the soles off my shoes, sit in a tree and learn to play the flute!

*(*MUDHEAD *reacts to what he sees ahead and steps audibly on the brakes.)*

MUDHEAD: Screeeeeesh!!

PORGIE: Hey! Watch it!

MUDHEAD: Wow! Look, Porgie! Where are you gonna graduate from?

PORGIE: Holy Mudhead, Mackerel! Morse Science High! It's disappeared!

(A climactic beat of movie music is suddenly broken off and all the lights go out. A beat. Then a voice:)

BEN BLAND: Technical difficulties are preventing the continuation of tonight's Ben Bland Foxhowl Feature, *High School Madness.* We are working on the problem...

(Still in the darkness, male VOICES *chant:)*

VOICES: Shoes for Industry! Shoes For The Dead! Shoes For Industry!

(Spotlit on the T V screen is JOE BEETS.*)*

JOE: Hi! I'm Joe Beets. Say, what chance does a returning deceased war veteran have for that good-paying job, more sugar and the free mule you've been dreaming of? Well, think it over. Then take off your shoes. Now you can see how increased spending opportunities means harder work for everyone, and more of it, too! So do your part today, Joe. Join with millions of your neighbors and turn in your shoes!

VOICES: For Industry!

(The T V screen goes black.)

BEN: Sorry, folks, but we have lost the picture portion of our pics-mission...ah... Oh!

(The picture returns. STUDENTS *are crowded around* MUDHEAD'S *jalopy. It's only moments later in the movie.)*

MUDHEAD: Jumpin' jujubes, Porgie! It looks like a wasteland! There's nothin' left but the flagpole!

PORGIE: I don't know what to say, Mudhead...

BOTTLES: *(Sidling up to him)* Hi, Mudhead...

MUDHEAD: *(Couldn't care less)* Oh, hi, Bottles.

BOTTLES: I know who did this! It was those bullies at Communist Martyrs High School, that's who!

PORGIE: Oh, come on, Bottles. We don't know who did it yet.

BOTTLES: I've got a very good idea!

ALVARADO: Hey, Porgie, you've got to help us!

(STUDENTS, *gathered around the jalopy make a great picture.*)

STUDENTS: Yeah! That's right!

ALVARADO: What do you think we should do?

PORGIE: Well, gee, I don't think we ought to jump to any conclusions or take a...

BOTTLES: Poop! Mudhead, Porgie! Principal Poop's on the radio!

STUDENTS: The Pooper? What...

PORGIE: Shhhh! Gather round, kids, and stay on camera! We'll all listen together!

(The STUDENTS *gather in a listening tableau as* POOP *appears at a downstage microphone.)*

POOP: ...All of us want to know, just as much as I want to know, who's responsible...

BOTTLES: Communist Martyrs High School, that's who!

POOP: And until we do, I must make my dirty— er—duty clean—ah—clear! And announce the suspendering of the upcoming graduating exercises which cannot—and will—which aren't taking place!

PORGIE: Oh, no! I'm never gonna graduate!

POOP: But don't worry! Don't worry. Your food, housing, insecurity will be guaranteed by your Department of Redundancy Department and the Natural Guard.

MUDHEAD: I bet they're gonna surround and protect us!

POOP: And remember, trusswrappers will be persecuted! So please, stay where you are! Don't move.

And don't panic. Don't take off your shoes! Jobs is on the way! Thank you. And now, here's a record I think you'll really dig...

(A 1950 hit spins. The STUDENTS *all gabble about what they've just heard.)*

PORGIE: Gollee! Hey, hold it down, kids! Don't get excited!

ALVARADO: Who's excited?

PORGIE: Listen, the only way we're gonna get the old school back is us! I've got a really swell idea...

(Once again, the T V goes dark. A light picks out GEORGE, *costumed as "Mr Liverface" in a bloodstained white smock. He confidently walks forward, stops and looks out.)*

GEORGE: Ah—is this my mark? ...Do I look alright? ...Thank you. Any time.

*(*GEORGE *waits for a cue, then sings a little jingle while* MOM *comes on.)*

"MR LIVERFACE": ...And I put 'em on the grocery wall!...

MOM: Mr. Liverface?

"MR LIVERFACE": Well, well, well! What can I do for you, m'am?

MOM: Mister Liverface, you're a butcher. You're up to your loins in fresh meat every day. What's the best food for my dog?

"MR LIVERFACE": Oh! What all dogs love to eat—cat!

MOM: Cat? Er, ha, ha, ha...

"MR LIVERFACE": I'm serious. There's enough protein and minerals in a teeny kitty's body to make a big dog happy and healthy. And there's a full dead cat in every can of "Mr. Liverface's Dead Cat Dog Food."

MOM: Well, that's all right for the little doggy, Mister L, but what do I feed my cat?

"MR LIVERFACE": Dog!

MOM: *(She hits him with her purse)* Not my dog!

"MR LIVERFACE": No, no, no, m'am! But there's a full pound of ground Pound Hound in every can of "Mr. Liverface's Dead Dog Cat Food."

MOM: I'll take one of each.

"MR LIVERFACE": You are one of each!

MOM: And one for Gramps. He's one too!

"MR LIVERFACE": *(He sings)*
Dogs and cats, and cats and dogs –
Your pets can eat them all!
I chop 'em up 'n' stuff 'em in a can,
And put 'em on the grocery wall!

(GEORGE holds in character for a moment, then nods.)

GEORGE: Good? Thank you... *(As he walks off, to himself)* Well, now I hope my SAG health benefits will kick in again.

(As GEORGE disappears, there's a big explosion. As it dies out, SERGEANT MUDHEADSKY, Korean War G I, rifle aimed, ducks into the room, ready for anything. He looks around, senses no danger, and calls out:)

MUDHEADSKY: Come on in, Lieutenant Tirebiter!

(LT TIREBITER, in camo, comes in with his pistol at the ready, looks carefully around, until he comes to GEORGE's refrigerator.)

LT TIREBITER: Think there's any food in that Gook icebox, Mudheadsky?

MUDHEADSKY: Gooks only eat groatcakes, Lieutenant.

LT TIREBITER: Doesn't everybody? Say! What happened to the recon team?

MUDHEADSKY: *(Yelling out the door)* Hey, Private! How long since Pico and Alvarado been out on patrol?

PRIVATE: *(Ducking his head in)* Since 1400, Sarge.

MUDHEADSKY: Geeze, that's two thousand years.

PRIVATE: I hope they can find their way back. I'm gettin' hungry.

(An airplane makes a low pass over the house. Everyone ducks. Cautiously, they relax again.)

MUDHEADSKY: Personally, I'm getting worried about Pico and Alvarado.

LT TIREBITER: Well, don't make a "Korea" out of it. *(He laughs, ruefully.)*

MUDHEADSKY: Don't let it get to you, sir.

LT TIREBITER: I'm alright, Mudheadsky. After all, those good ol' boys fought their way out of East L A—they can find their way back into Gook Valley, right?

PRIVATE: Sarge! Lieutenant! Somethin's movin' out in the woods.

LT TIREBITER: Where?

PRIVATE: Sector R.

LT TIREBITER: Give 'em the password, Sarge.

MUDHEADSKY: Yeah. I'd better disguise my voice. *(He moves to the door and calls out in a bad Japanese dialect.)* Heya, Joe! Who wonna Secon' Worl' War, you so smart?

(From way off, the voices of PICO and ALVARADO yell:)

PICO: Not responsible!

ALVARADO: Park and lock it!

PRIVATE: It's O K, sir. That's Pico and Alvarado awright!

MUDHEADSKY: *(Calling)* Come on in, boys! And hey! Don't run in the trenches!

(PICO and ALVARADO, blissed out draftees, are from a 'Nam war movie. They run in, decorated with tropical hats and souvenirs.)

ALVARADO: Hi, you guys!

PICO: Hey, Mr. Lieutenant!

LT TIREBITER: Stand easy, men.

ALVARADO: I am easy!

PICO: Yeah! Standing is easy. Comedy is hard!

ALVARADO: That's right!

LT TIREBITER: How was it out there?

PICO: Weird! We been shootin' Reds and Yellows all day.

ALVARADO: Hoo, boy! Am I sleepy!

(ALVARADO settles comfortably in GEORGE's recliner. PICO starts to rummage around in the refrigerator.)

LT TIREBITER: What about the Gooks?

PICO: Bad news, Lieutenant! There're Gooks all around here.

(PICO discovers GEORGE's little baggie of 'shrooms and pockets it.)

ALVARADO: They live here, Lieutenant. They've got women and pigs and gardens and everything!

PICO: I was talkin' to this one little Gook...

ALVARADO: I was talkin' to his daughter! She's got the biggest...

LT TIREBITER: You know we've got orders to surround these little Gooks?

ALVARADO: That'll be easy. There's millions of them on all three sides of us.

PICO: Yeah, they live here, Lieutenant! They've got women and pigs and gardens and everything!

LT TIREBITER: That means we've got those little Gooks right where we want them, right?

PICO: Yeah! And tonight's the Planting Moon, so every one of them is going to be out wading in the paddies.

ALVARADO: Me too!

MUDHEADSKY: This sounds like a perfect set-up. What are we gonna *do*, Lieutenant?

PICO: What *are* we gonna do, Lieutenant?

ALVARADO: *What* are we gonna do, Lieutenant?

LT TIREBITER: All right, men. We're gonna deploy at 0800.

MUDHEADSKY: Check.

LT TIREBITER: Recon all L O M Sectors.

PRIVATE: *(Leaving)* Czech!

LT TIREBITER: Bring up the 455s.

PICO: Pole!

LT TIREBITER: Locate our fire parameters.

ALVARADO: Bohunk!

LT TIREBITER: Make a clean sweep. Flush out the enemy and ki-ki-ki-um...

MUDHEADSKY: What's that, sir?

PICO: Sir? Excuse me? Lieutenant? Sir?

ALVARADO: What are we gonna *do*, man?

PICO: Yeah! After we flush 'em out!

LT TIREBITER: We're going to lock and load, Private, and we're going to go out there and ki... ki...

(LT TIREBITER *can't say it. The word sticks in his craw. The movie actors start to fall apart.*)

ALVARADO: Is that after we lock and load?

PICO: You mean, after we rock and roll!

LT TIREBITER: We're gonna ki-ki-ki...

ALVARADO: Kick 'em?

MUDHEADSKY: Take it easy, sir. Listen, it's not your fault.

LT TIREBITER: Ki-ki-ki-ki...

PICO: Cuddle 'em?

MUDHEADSKY: What are you trying to say, Porge? George?

LT TIREBITER: Cut!

(*That ends the "take." An* ASSISTANT DIRECTOR *strides officiously on set.*)

ASSISTANT DIRECTOR: Cut! Cut! Save the lights! Reset!

(*The other actors look variously disgruntled, bored or frustrated and leave the set. The lights on set go down and up on the T V screen, revealing* DARLENE, *holding up a gaudy dress. And off-stage* VOICE OVER *says:*)

VOICE OVER: Comedienne Mrs. Arlene Yukamoto of Pine Barren, New Jersey, doesn't know our Napalmolive camera is focused on her!

ARLENE: *(Highly edited)* No! It's true. You see—my husband is a policeman, and you wouldn't believe how dirty he gets my clothes. It mean it. It's unbelievable.

VOICE OVER: Oh, but we believed Mrs P Q, and listen to her reaction!

ARLENE: I worry about it all night sometimes, you know? I hate to admit it. Look at this horrible stain. Sometimes I think my kids are doing it on purpose!

(A siren sounds and a costumed figure appears.)

SERGEANT: Nothin's on purpose, ma'm!

ARLENE: Who are you?

SERGEANT: Sgt. Schvinkter of the Dirt Patrol! Our mission, to keep America clean! And when the job gets this dirty, there's only one weapon! New Napalmolive, with Killer Enzy...

(The T V screen goes dark on the commercial. The High School movie's next reel is rolling. PORGIE and MUDHEAD sneak into the set.

MUDHEAD: *(Whispering)* That was a stupid idea, Porgie! Here we are at Commie Martyrs, but how are we gonna find Morse Science High?

PORGIE: Well, let's get out of Exposition Park, Mudhead, and we'll be all right. Come on—this way...

MUDHEAD: You go first! Stop shoving!...

(But PORGIE is ahead of MUDHEAD, going for the refrigerator. Is someone behind him?

MUDHEAD: Hey...Porgie...?

PORGIE: What?

MUDHEAD: I ain't afraid, but it sure its sp-sp-spooky in here!

PORGIE: That's because we're on the Other Side. *(He discovers something, which he pulls out from behind the fridge.)*

MUDHEAD: Yeah, must be. Hey, what's that?

PORGIE: Looks like a picture... Hey, leggo of my pants!

MUDHEAD: Porge...

PORGIE: What?

MUDHEAD: I'm not holding on to your pants!

PORGIE: You're not?

MUDHEAD: No...

PORGIE: Oh, no!

(BOTTLES *has been here all along! She steps out from behind the fridge.*)

BOTTLES: Hi, boys.

PORGIE: Bottles! How did you get in here?

BOTTLES: Oh, I have my ways.

MUDHEAD: I bet you gave the guard a sleeve job.

BOTTLES: Oh, yeah? That's what you guys are always thinking about!

PORGIE: Quiet!

BOTTLES: You just come over here and I'll show you something!

MUDHEAD: Don't you trust her, Porgie. Then she'll want to see yours!

PORGIE: No, Mudhead. She's right. Look!

(BOTTLES *holds up the large framed photo of* POOP, *which had been resting by the fridge.*)

BOTTLES: You see? You see what I've found?

MUDHEAD: By golly, it's him!

PORGIE: The Commies have got the big portrait of Principal Poop that used to hang in the Boy's Supreme Court at Morse Science!

MUDHEAD: Those eyes. Weird!

(*From off stage, the sound of whistling.*)

PORGIE: Shhh! It's one of them! I'll carry the ball! You guys be quiet.

MUDHEAD: Be cool, Porge. Be cool!

(ALVARADO *saunters on, wearing a "Che" T-shirt.*)

ALVARADO: Hiya, kiddo!

PORGIE: Er... Shoes For Industry, compadre!

ALVARADO: Yeah, sure. Hey, are you guys holding?

PORGIE: Gosh, no. The means of production are held by all the people.

ALVARADO: No, man! You know, you got any uppers?

PORGIE: Uppers? Gosh, no. There are no classes in our society.

MUDHEAD: Or in our High School!

BOTTLES: Quiet, stupid!

ALVARADO: Come on, baby. You can tell me. You got any pot?

PORGIE: Oh, no, not yet. But soon, Heavy Industry will make it possible for all the People to have everything it desires in a Free Marketplace.

BOTTLES: That's right, yes.

ALVARADO: Oh, daddy-o! You guys are so crazy! *(Leaving, he sings:)* Crazy, man, crazy! Crazy, man, crazy! What are you gonna do...?

MUDHEAD: Gosh! You really convinced him we were O K, comrade—er, I mean, Porgie.

BOTTLES: *(Starting to leave)* That sure was a close one. We better get out of here!

PORGIE: No, no, no. Wait a minute, Bottles. They must be hiding Morse Science around here someplace. They've got the Pooper's picture.

MUDHEAD: They've got everybody's picture!

BOTTLES: Well, they're not going to get mine! I'm leaving! *(She walks off the set, past the fridge.)*

PORGIE: Gee, now we'll have to go after her! Come on, Mudhead.

MUDHEAD: O K... Alright...

(As they follow BOTTLES, *they see what is hidden off stage and stop in surprise.)*

PORGIE: Mudhead! Look! We've found it!

MUDHEAD: Wow! Your old Alma Mater. It's been taken apart and stacked up and—look, everything's labeled!

*(*MUDHEAD *goes off, leaving* PORGIE *to gape.)*

PORGIE: This has never happened to any other High School ever before!

MUDHEAD: *(From off)* Hey, Porgie! I found something really big!

PORGIE: What is it?

MUDHEAD: *(Returning, reading)* The label says, Number 11478, *High School Madness,* Mural, Auditorium, Right Rear. "Heroic Struggle of the Little Guys to finish the Mural."

PORGIE: That's ours, alright. I guess we've got these Reds red-handed!

MUDHEAD: *(He's found one)* Yeah! Here's a Red Hand!

PORGIE: Well, we have to take it along for evidence. And I'll take...

(There, waiting for PORGIE, *is a pair of bright blue gym shorts, with a tag attached. He grabs them and turns to leave.)*

PORGIE: ...this and then we'll go back and tell everybody...

(A sudden dramatic musical chord!)

PORGIE: Oh, no!

*(*DAD *appears on the screen, then enters the set.)*

DAD: Hold it right there, boys!

MUDHEAD: Mister Tirebiter!

PORGIE: Dad!

DAD: "Dad, sir!" to you, son. I'm People's
Commissioner Tirebiter now. And... *(Striding up to*
PORGIE*)* nobody's sweetheart! *(Sucker-punches him)*

PORGIE: *(From the floor)* Ow! Gosh, you must've stolen
the election, Dad!

DAD: Right, son! Now I *am* The People. And The
People—us—wants me to tell them— *(Gesturing to*
the audience) —You! Just what you're doing with your
hands in... *(He takes the garment from* PORGIE, *admires it,*
then shakes his head and reads the label.) Auction lot 35729
comma Shorts comma One Pair Blue Gym comma
slash Protector, worn by *(Impressed)* Barbara Bobeau!

PORGIE: Oh, no!

(Everyone holds his position for a moment. The
ASSISTANT DIRECTOR comes on.

ASSISTANT DIRECTOR: Cut! Print! Very nice, everybody.
Take Five. Courtroom Scene is next. Stage B.

(The cast breaks away. Lights dim on the set. On the
T V screen, with a burst of news music, appears a flashy
newsreader, DAWN.*)*

DAWN: Coming up on U T V's Hour of the Wolf's
Headlines at Dawn, next, with me, Dawn Headline,
today's rumors behind the News: Big Light Slated to
appear in East! U S Government to merge with former
Zinc Bushing company! And, there's hamburger
all over the Highway in Mystic, Connecticut. I'll be
believable, after this...

(Then, just as if someone had channel-switched, we are
back on the set of High School Madness. Or is it Parallel
Hell? It's been slightly reset to resemble a courtroom. The
ASSISTANT DIRECTOR. *marches in with a clapstick.)*

ASSISTANT DIRECTOR: Alright, people. Let's get it right
the first time! This is the Court Martial scene. Places!

(PORGIE *looks around, confused.*)

ASSISTANT DIRECTOR: George! Places!

(The other actors take their opening positions. POOP is the Judge, DAD the Attorney. PORGIE realizes he's in another movie and slips his camo jacket on over his high school sweater. At this point the older GEORGE enters and looks on.)

ASSISTANT DIRECTOR: *(Claps the stick)* Take One! Action!

LT TIREBITER: Look, I told you, I can't remember. I know it's my line, but I can't remember...

DAD: George! George! Your whole defense rests on your remembering what you said...

LT TIREBITER: Look, Judge Poop—everything went black!

DAD: Don't overact, George!

POOP: It's painfully obvious this man is in no condition to replay the scene in question. Will the A D read the script back to him?

ASSISTANT DIRECTOR: Yes, sir. *(He reads from the filmscript)* Alvarado: "Sir, what are we gonna do, man?" Lieutenant: "We're going to go out there and ki-ki-ki-cut! I'm sorry, but I can't say it." Zzzzzt, beep! End of reel.

POOP: What happened, George?

LT TIREBITER: Look, Poop—when I signed my contract with this outfit, I fully intended to fulfill its terms with honor, sir. But you never told me I had to go out there and kill anybody. My conscience wouldn't let me...

POOP: *(Banging his gavel)* Conscience! Tirebiter, we will not tolerate the use of Prohibited Language in this courts-martial!

DAD: You could be blacklisted for that, George!

POOP: The accursed will be advised of the absence of his rights under the Secret Code of Military Toughness and will act accordingly.

(LT TIREBITER starts to say something when the ASSISTANT DIRECTOR comes on with his clapstick.)

ASSISTANT DIRECTOR: Oyez, oyez! We're ready to roll on the Courtroom Scene, Take One! Places!

(Everyone on the set looks at LT TIREBITER. He is, of course, the same actor who is playing PORGIE.)

ASSISTANT DIRECTOR: George! Places!

(The older GEORGE starts to move in, but the young LT TIREBITER shrugs off his camo jacket to reveal PORGIE's High School sweater. He crosses the set to take his place beside DAD, who has moved to a new start position. The ASSISTANT DIRECTOR is impatient.)

ASSISTANT DIRECTOR: Are we ready? Action! Take One!

PORGIE: I'd like to take one, too, Dad.

DAD: Scared, son? Don't be. I love you at times like this!

PORGIE: I know, Dad, I know. But how can you be in two places at once, when, well, you're... I mean, Dad! I still don't see how you can be my defense lawyer and the People's Prosecutor at the same time.

DAD: Easy, son. This way I can personally see that you're persecuted to the full extent of the laws!

PORGIE: That's my Dad...

(The JUDGE pounds his gavel.)

PORGIE: Gee whiz! I'm sorry!

DAD: I suppose it's we Parents who should be "sorry," Judge. We've failed somewhere.

JUDGE: It's not our fault any more, Mister Prosecution. Call the next witness.

DAD: What do you think I ought to call him, Judge?

POOP: Well, I don't know. He doesn't have a name. It seems he never went to school.

DAD: Well, then—the People calls to the stand...you!

ALVARADO: *(From out in the house)* Don't point at me, daddy-o, or I'll cut off your finger!

POOP: No, no. You. Over there.

DAD: The man with no shoes!

MUDHEAD: Who, me?

DAD & POOP: You!

PORGIE: Mudhead? Gollee, Dad!

(POOP bangs his gavel. The ASSISTANT DIRECTOR brings MUDHEAD a script to swear on.)

ASSISTANT DIRECTOR: You promise to covet property, propriety, plurality, surety, security, and not hurt the State? Say "what".

MUDHEAD: What?

ASSISTANT DIRECTOR: Take your stand.

DAD: Now then, Mister—ah, Head...

MUDHEAD: Hi, Mister Tirebiter! You know me!

DAD: Do you know the defendant?

MUDHEAD: Do I know Porgie? Sure!

DAD: And you spend all your free time with him?

MUDHEAD: Except when he's in school.

DAD: So you don't go to school?

MUDHEAD: Heck no! I'm thirty years old!

DAD: But you were in school, weren't you?

MUDHEAD: Never!

DAD: And with your friend Porgie?

MUDHEAD: No!

DAD: Last night?

MUDHEAD: Oh, you mean at Commie Martyrs!

DAD: Communist Martyrs High School, exactly!

MUDHEAD: Well, yeah, of course. Porgie had to find out where they were hiding Morse Science, or he couldn't get out.

DAD: Or he couldn't get out! He admits it! My son was trying to get out!

MUDHEAD: Isn't everybody?

DAD: To get out in times of Declared Emergency!

MUDHEAD & PORGIE: What emergency?

DAD: Well, there you are, Judge Poop. Youth here doesn't seem to know about the disappearance of the Old School.

MUDHEAD: But that's what Porgie was looking for!

POOP: *(Banging his gavel)* If you don't answer the question, young man, we're going to have to gag you.

MUDHEAD: What question?

POOP: Gag him!

DAD: Who was that lady I saw you with last night?

MUDHEAD: That was no lady, that was Bottles!

POOP: Bottles? You found them with bottles?

(GEORGE *has seen enough. He enters the stage unobserved and takes the uniform camo jacket from where the* LT TIREBITER *left it to become* PORGIE.)

DAD: You see, Judge Poop? He's a good boy gone bad. He moves when he's told not to move. He takes off his shoes to evade the men who are trying to protect him. They sneak into a forbidden sector after curfew, where

I caught them with their hands up something they don't belong!

PORGIE: But, Dad...

DAD: Your friends at Commie Martyrs must be mighty proud of you!

PORGIE: Dad, I don't have any friends at Commie Martyrs.

MUDHEAD: I've never ever seen anyone from there!

PORGIE: You're right, Mudhead, and besides, there's no room for anybody there, anyway, because it's all filled up with Morse Science!

(GEORGE *slips on the jacket and steps forward in the character of* LT TIREBITER. PORGIE *looks at him in surprise. The others don't seem to notice.*)

GEORGE/LT TIREBITER: *(To* PORGIE*)* You got *that* right, kid. Now, hold the thought.

(PORGIE *drops back to watch and* GEORGE *confronts* POOP.*)*

GEORGE/LT TIREBITER: Sure, Poop! Bottles! I got so I'd drink anything and marry anybody. Then I couldn't seem to get off the stuff. My whole career went up in smoke. There was no way I could follow the scenario written by the people who pay for your wheelchairs, General.

(*The* ASSISTANT DIRECTOR *comes in, carrying a decorated military camo jacket and hands it to* POOP.*)*

POOP: Are you impugning, sir, that this uniform might be for sale? This uniform, that bears the three stars that indicate my ratings? Bedecked with ribbons that resents—er—represents every theater of war?

(POOP *gives the jacket back to the* ASSISTANT DIRECTOR, *who models it in various movie poses.*)

POOP: Who wore it last, in our proud company? *(He reads the tag)* This full-dress uniform, W-dash-2565, seen in *Our Finest Hours*...

GEORGE: *(Aside to* PORGIE*)* What a dog.

POOP: ...in *Ruthless Combat*...

GEORGE: What happened to Ruth?

PORGIE: *(Getting in the game)* B-movie for sure...

POOP: ...in *Dogfights Over Broadway*...

GEORGE & PORGIE: That was a musical!

POOP: ...and worn out, finally, here, on this spot, in *Parallel Hell*! What is it worth? What do I hear?

ALVARADO: *(From out in the House)* That's metaphysically absurd, man! How could I know what you hear?

GEORGE/LT TIREBITER: I'll buy it! Five dollars!

POOP: I heard that! What do you think you're trying to do, Lieutenant? Buy your way out of these proceedings?

GEORGE/LT TIREBITER: I am out! I don't like you, I don't like your script and I don't want any part in what you're selling here! And I'm walking off your set!

DAD & POOP: You can't do that!

GEORGE/LT TIREBITER: Just watch me...

POOP: You'll never work in this town again, Tirebiter!

GEORGE/LT TIREBITER: What town?

(He starts to go, but realizes he still has to help out PORGIE, *who is trapped in his own movie. He calls him over. The movies are now hopelessly intertwined.)*

GEORGE/LT TIREBITER: Kid! Hey, kid! Remember how Commie Martyrs was so full of Morse Science there was no room for the kids? Where did all the kids go?

PORGIE: Gosh! Where *did* all the kids go?

DAD: They're in Korea!

GEORGE/LT TIREBITER & PORGIE: On which side?

ALVARADO: *(Still out in the audience)* What do you *mean* by that?

PORGIE: I mean...

GEORGE/LT TIREBITER: ...In whose movie?

POOP: This is no movie. This is real!

GEORGE/LT TIREBITER: Which reel?

(The ASSISTANT DIRECTOR hands POOP a large film can.)

POOP: *(Reading the label)* This reel! The last reel of this vintage motion picture, *High School Madness*, Lot Number M dash 25. Metrocolor. 35 millimeter. Now, who started at five dollars?

(PORGIE looks at GEORGE, who shrugs off the camo jacket and gives it to PORGIE, who doesn't put it on yet. Silently POOP carries on the auction of the studio properties, carried away by the rest of the cast.)

PORGIE: Right. I guess it was me.

MUDHEAD: Porgie, what are you doing?

PORGIE: It's all a fake, Mudhead. They lied to me.

GEORGE: Who do you mean, "they"?

PORGIE: You know, "them".

GEORGE: Name three.

PORGIE: Well first there was my Dad...

GEORGE & MUDHEAD: Yeah...

PORGIE: And then there was the Pooper...

GEORGE: Right so far...

PORGIE: And then there was... *(He slips the camo jacket on again.)*

GEORGE: You?

PORGIE: Me...

GEORGE: Nice goin', kid. See you around.

(GEORGE, *once again his old age, walks off. For a beat we can hear the auction continue.*)

POOP: Let's go to 25 bid—25 bid, now 30, now 35, thank you, sir. Go to 50—go to a half—37.50, thank you miss... *(Silent)*

MUDHEAD: Hey, Porge—whose movie is this anyway?

PORGIE: It's nobody's now, Mudhead. I'm getting out!

MUDHEAD: How're you gonna do it, Porge?

PORGIE: I don't know...

MUDHEAD: How did you get in here?

PORGIE: I don't remember...

MUDHEAD: Where were you before?

PORGIE: Before what?

MUDHEAD: Before this scene!

PORGIE: Right! That was before...before I...

(Once again, the channel changes. GEORGE's room has been rearranged into a game-show set from the Seventies. PORGIE, in a quick change assisted by one of the SOLD-OUT GIRLS, becomes the show host DANNY DOLLAR. One of the GIRLS assists an overwhelmed, staggering MRS PRESKY into the spotlight. Show music is "groovy.")

DANNY: ...Sold Out!

(The GIRLS chime in with a musical echo of the most important words in DANNY's pitches.)

GIRLS: S-o-o-o-o-o-l-l-l-d-d-d O-o-u-u-t!

DANNY: With me, Danny Dollar! And that's right, Mrs Caroline Presky, you've Sold Out! So, let's see

what you've won so far on this, your third week on
Hawaiian Sell-Out!

GIRLS: Hiiiii-wwwiiii-annnnn Sellllll-out!

(The GIRLS *demo her winnings using a variety of objects
still around the kitchen, finally parading and posing around
the fridge. Poor* MRS PRESKY *can't believe any of this.)*

DANNY: Let's take a look at Mrs Presky's Heap so far.
Wow! A complete set of color bars for Mrs. P's new
home, some leveled mountain skis and water-rollers
for that fun-filled open season, an unattached Grid-
5 Stand-Up Re-heater with the Smoke Window, and
now...

(The GIRLS *do a Ziegfeld pose and intone:)*

GIRLS: Ch-e-e-e-ffff An-n-n-n-toin-eee!

DANNY: Three-hundred full pounds of Chef Antoine's
Southern Fried Glimps, toasted to Golden Perfection.
cubed, reheated and returned to water before you're
ready, Mrs P!

MRS PRESKY: Ohhhh...

DANNY: And on the inside?

(The GIRLS *open the refrigerator door.)*

DANNY: Well, look at this! It's just as lovely! Two
shelves where none are needed! And take a peek at
that! Close the door and the light stays on!

(As the GIRLS *close the door, there's a big music cue.)*

DANNY: Fantastic, right? Unbelievable! So, Mrs Presky,
tell us, how do you feel?

MRS PRESKY: Ah...sick...

(The GIRLS *cluster around* MRS PRESKY.)*

DANNY: Well, you can afford to be sick now, love! But
like the Good Book says, there's bigger deals to come!

GIRLS: Bigggger deeee-allls to C-ooooooommmmm!

(MRS PRESKY *collapses into the* GIRLS' *arms.*)

DANNY: And here's your last Sell-Out, Mrs Presky. Which would you rather do? Hit Danny over the head with a bag of sugar or beat out that rhythm on a drum?

(The GIRLS *harmonize on "Bag of Sugar" and "on a drum".)*

(MRS PRESKY can't decide. There's the Tropical Beach Bag and there's the Exotic Drum and there's DANNY *and the* GIRLS *are chanting.)*

GIRLS: Bag! ...Drum! ...Bag! ...Drum!

MRS PRESKY: I...I don't know...I suppose...well...I'll take...the bag!

(The GIRLS *cheer and then pull things out of the fridge.)*

DANNY: You mean you're going to trade this four-foot cube of solid 18-carat Swiss bullion—and the snake knives, Mrs. Presky? All for this little bag?

GIRLS: Sheee-eee w-a-aa-nn-tt-ss the B—A-A-A-G!

(At this moment, GEORGE *reappears in his "at home" bathrobe and regards the situation sleepily. It was his show. It was awful. He searches for his remote.)*

MRS PRESKY: Well, yes. I want the bag.

DANNY: All right then. Here it is. Open it up!

(MRS PRESKY takes the bag from one of the GIRLS *and opens it. She can't believe what she sees.)*

MRS PRESKY: Why...why...this is a bag of shit!

DANNY: Yes, but it's really great shit, Mrs. Presky...

(GEORGE finds and uses his remote. Hawaiian Sell-Out vanishes. A succession of television images and bits of programs follow as he clicks from channel to channel.)

DR MATH: ...at's 2 Postmen, times 3 Animal Control Officers, divided by 2 Gassed Meter Readers, makes

how many Bendable Integrated Community Workers?
Decode your answer now... Did you remember to carry
the Bum? Good! The answer...

(GEORGE *clicks to the affable Morning Hosts:*)

PATTI: ...nd that's why he's so mean!

HUGH: Great story, Patti...

PATTI: What else happened in History today, Hugh?

HUGH: In History, Patti? Well, today, of course is the
38th of Cunegonde, and on this day in 1-9-3-8-B-C, Patti,
Mr. George Antrobus invented the wheel.

PATTI: Just in time! And in 1889, the Peace of Humus
broke out, ending the Hundred Years War Against the
Cows.

HUGH: And last year, Patti, you and the viewers will be
interested in noting that the World ended.

PATTI: As we know it, Hugh.

HUGH: You're darn tootin', Patti.

PATTI: I sure am!

HUGH: Say, who was born today?

PATTI: Nobody, Hugh.

HUGH: I mean in History, Patti. Before they changed
the water.

(*Things are getting worse out there.* GEORGE *sits in his
recliner and clicks again.*)

BOB BASELINE: Let's talk about your car. It's screaming
"Wash Me Please!" Now, if you're a Mister Common
Sense, you won't believe me when I tell you that I've
got an envelope that'll clean your car while you're
driving home to work!

(*Another click reveals:*)

MISS AMES: That's right, friends! Ed aims to please and so does Louise! So don't hide arms, get side arms! At Ames Guns! 20102 East Rhode Island School of Design Terrace in Yukaipa!

(And another:)

BOB BASELINE: ...can believe me this time, George! This is nothing like those Austrian self-sharpening razors...

(The channels and commercials are blending.)

PATTI: And you see here, Hugh? This one won't take over the house like the high-speed vibrating clocks...

(GEORGE lies back and closes his eyes. The channels keep flipping.)

BOB BASELINE: So don't change...

MADGE: You don't have to change...

HUGH: Had enough?

PATTI: Seen enough?

MISS AMES: Oh, Daddy! Where can I get a good deal in a Righteous Atmosphere?

(With a burst of organ music, in a Cloud of Glory, SISTER FLASH reappears. She has the Bag.)

SISTER FLASH: Right here, dear friends! Right here! God almighty, I'm full of it! But I'm going to let it go. And you've got to let it go. Because, dear friends, just as sure as you can bet it, one of those two Greatest Guys Up There is going to let go, just as you are letting go. Ahhhhhhh... Isn't that a load off your mind. I know it is off mine.

(SISTER FLASH over to GEORGE's chair, opens it, speaks, then sets the bag on the floor beside it. He still snoozes.)

SISTER FLASH: Don't be afraid. Look at it! Just look at that steaming heap of plot-buttered goat custards... *(As she goes)* My, my, my...

(SISTER FLASH *slips away. It's dawn. The phone rings.* GEORGE *awakes and answers it.)*

GEORGE: Hello... Good morning? This is George Tirebiter.

(The light picks up his agent, MARIE, *on her end of the phone. She's very young by* GEORGE's *standards.)*

MARIE: Good morning, Georgie. How's the old man today?

GEORGE: Well, I'm a bit worn out, actually. Who is this?

MARIE: Don't you remember me, George? Marie? Your agent? Four Star Hopeless Former Celebrity Management?

GEORGE: Oh, yes. You're the new one. Well, Marie, my news is, I've been up all night, watching myself on television. Two great 1950s classics—*Parallel Hell!* and *High School Mad...*

MARIE: There's no ten percent in old movies, George.

GEORGE: No ninety-percent either, dear. What can I do for you?

MARIE: No, George. It's what can Four Star Hopeless do for you. The phones have been ringing off the hook all morning. Seems you're wanted.

GEORGE: Really? No one's wanted me in years. Who called?

MARIE: Well, George, these aren't from Spielberg or Pixar...

GEORGE: It's not that mattress company again, is it? "Unconscious Village"? They want to steal everybody's dreams...

(Off in the distance, the sound of approaching ice cream wagon bells.)

MARIE: Nope, no commercials. Do you know a Mister Sennett?

GEORGE: Only Mack.

MARIE: How about a Buster Somebody?

GEORGE: Well, Buster Keaton...

MARIE: Babe Hardy? Stan Jefferson?

GEORGE: That's Laurel and Hardy...

MARIE: Must be a stand-up act. How about a Mister Dunkerfield? He said he'd rather be in Philadelphia, whatever that means.

GEORGE: *(Imitating Fields)* "Yes, yes, I'd rather be in Philadelphia!" That's W C!

MARIE: You remember him, George?

GEORGE: Of course! I remember them all! Was there anyone else?

MARIE: A Mister Fetchit. He said to tell you, "I's comin' Georgie, I's comin'!" Then there was a weird HONK! HONK! He didn't say anything else.

GEORGE: He never did...

MARIE: And Charlie no-last-name and—this'll kill ya!— Mr. Roach!

GEORGE: Hal Roach? I thought he was dead.

MARIE: Funny—he said the same thing about you.

(Those bells have gotten much louder. They seem to have stopped just outside the door.)

GEORGE: Can you wait just a moment, my dear? I haven't eaten in days, and I hear an ice cream wagon right outside...

MARIE: Whatever, George. I'll hold.

(GEORGE sets down the phone, goes up to the screen and looks out.)

GEORGE: I'm so hungry! Thank goodness someone finally came up into the Hills. *(He shrugs off his bathrobe as if molting an old skin and steps through the screen.)* Hey! Hey! Wait for me...

(GEORGE walks into the fresh dawn light outside.)

GEORGE: *(His voice becoming that of a young boy)* Hey, Mister! I've got a nickel! Wait for me! Wait for me!...

(Waving, GEORGE runs off to the light and the sound of the bells. Then all the lights fade slowly to black out.)

END OF PLAY

www.ingramcontent.com/pod-product-compliance
Lightning Source LLC
Chambersburg PA
CBHW070033110426
42741CB00035B/2752